I0441645

The Word "Toe"

MIKE BARDI

THE WORD "TOE"

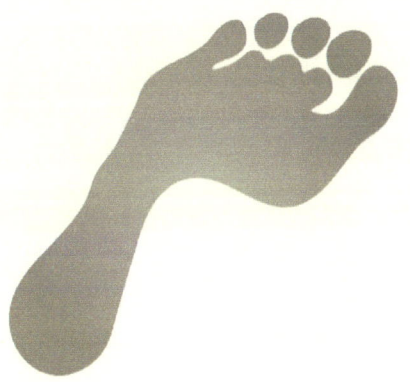

Copyright © 2015 Project Toe LLC

All rights reserved

To my lovely Mother,
you will be greatly missed.

CONTENTS

INTRODUCTION

"If you want to find the best ideas that could change the world, look no further than the graveyard." —Anonymous

As a child I always struggled to effectively communicate what was on my mind to another individual. I knew what I wanted to say, but I couldn't find the words to say it. My communication problem left me feeling frustrated, but also ashamed because I knew I had a problem that the other people in my life didn't seem to have. I did everything possible to hide the issue, but it took years of speech therapy for me to overcome my problem. Now that I'm older and more mature, I realize my urge to hide my problem was not unusual since I came to realize that we as humans are adept at masking our own struggles. Whether facing an addiction, depression, or even a moment of sadness caused by an event, we are superb at bluffing our way through—even if it's at our own expense.

It is much easier to use coping skills than it is to

admit you have a problem and to ask others for help. But for those who do reach out to friends or family for assistance, they typically get one of the following outcomes:

1. Friends and family comfort and support the person throughout the whole process.
2. Friends and family think the person has "problems," which may result in the loss of their respect or friendship.
3. Friends and family comfort the person for a little while until they decide the person has "problems," which may result in the loss of their respect or friendship.

This fear of losing the respect or love of someone close keeps many troubled people from asking for help from loved ones. Some others have relied on "the system" to help them when they were experiencing difficulties. Often, however, the system does not yield the hoped for results. Mental-health budgets are being cut and depression is rising, yet the number of people seeking help is on the decline.[1] There's a storm coming and there aren't enough umbrellas to go around.

Fortunately, there is an alternative called "social therapy." It's about empowering people who have endured a life struggle to help others who are currently going through the same problem. With this goal of connecting those in need with those who want to help, we started Project Toe—an organization empowering people to help others through a life struggle.

In the chapters ahead, I'd like to take you on the journey of Project Toe—how we started, the transitions we made along the way, and what the future holds for us (and how you might be able to help).

---

[1] World Health Organization.

1

DAYTONA BEACH

In 2010, while I was attending school at Embry-Riddle University in Florida, my friend Kayla came to visit for the week. Kayla was going through a difficult time in her life. She was recovering from self-harm while trying to overcome some past memories that were still haunting her.

One day while walking on the beach, Kayla became upset about some of the negative thoughts and emotions that she was feeling that had triggered her to self-harm a few days prior. When I asked why she didn't contact me when she was feeling troubled, she said the following words that would stick with me forever:

"Because I don't want to lose the people closest to me."

The thought being, if we put too much pressure on our friends and family, it may cause them to view us in a different light and to lose respect for us. They may not love us the way they once did, making us feel inadequate.

It's not as simple as asking someone for help. We as humans need to feel connected to each other; it's an important part of what makes us human. The difficulty is that in asking for help, we put ourselves in an extremely vulnerable position, when it would be easier to just suppress our feelings in hopes that they will eventually go away. When we wake up each day to realize they haven't, we find ourselves alone and afraid. These feelings of loneliness and fear are often what cause us to fall into unhealthy habits.

Kayla and I decided to try an experiment. Whenever she was feeling down and felt like she had no one to turn to, she would text me a neutral word that we had agreed to beforehand. This word had to be one that was easy to text and didn't have any direct connection to asking for help. We happened to be walking on the beach at the time and while looking at our sandy feet, we asked ourselves, "Why not 'toe?'" It's only three letters, it's easy to text, and it doesn't have any direct connection to asking for help. From that day forward, whenever she was feeling the urge to self-harm, she would text me the word "toe." This text would indicate to me in a non-confrontational way that she was asking for help. After she texted me, I'd stop whatever I was doing and simply text her back. Sometimes our conversations would be about whatever was on her mind, other times they were about something completely unrelated. The point was that it was a distraction for her until the urge for her to self-harm passed.

We restricted the conversations to texting in order to lower the barrier to communication. Many people, especially teens, prefer to articulate what's on their mind via text as opposed to voicing their concerns. Kayla could still call me if she wanted to, however, she was more comfortable with texting.

Our little experiment proved to be extremely helpful for us; so helpful, in fact, we thought others could benefit from the same idea. We imagined an entire world of people out there going through a similar situation who also might benefit from our little experiment. We had stumbled on an idea we believed in that also had the power to help others. We knew that we had to share it, but the question was, how? This idea worked well for us because Kayla had a resource that wasn't present before, and I felt by taking action that I could help her in some way, resulting in my feeling good about myself since I could make a small difference to her; it was a win-win for the both of us. If Kayla and I could experience these emotions, why couldn't others experience the same regardless of age, gender or location?

The initial thought was simply to spread the idea on self-harm forums for others to read about. After doing some research, however, we realized that we could do so much more. Instead of simply sharing the idea, we could build our own support network around self-harm—a network that would allow others to text us when they needed help.

We decided to test this idea using Google Voice. In case you've never heard of Google Voice, it's a service that provides you with one number for multiple phones. Most importantly for us, it allowed us to send and receive texts from one number. With a little help, we could promote this phone number for others to text in whenever they were feeling down or had an urge to self-harm. Google Voice worked perfectly for our needs at the time since it was free to use and would give us the ability to validate our idea to see if others would actually use our service. With this phone number, we hoped to start a support network for those suffering with self-harm. They could text in whenever they wanted, without necessarily having to speak to someone verbally, which they would have to do if they used a traditional hotline. We viewed this idea as a hybrid between a peer support network and a crisis hotline—a peer support network because we weren't professionals or trained to offer support and a crisis hotline because anyone could text us when they urgently felt the need. With our Google Voice number in place, it was now time to tell others to text "toe."

2

TEXT "TOE"

Whenever someone had the urge to self-harm, that person would text "toe" to our number and one of the Project Toe volunteers would respond. Little did anyone know that it was only Kayla and I responding to texts in the beginning.

We now needed to get the word out about the project. We didn't have much money, so our only marketing plan was to see if bloggers would be kind enough to promote us for free on their YouTube channel. I recall spending hours sending out personal messages to YouTube bloggers in hopes one would respond with positive feedback. After several failed attempts, one person responded with the magic words, "Of course I'd promote you guys!"

The blogger's pen name is IdrankTheSeaWater; she later preferred to be called Melissa C. Water. She's the author of a book called *Lady Injury* and an avid YouTube blogger promoting awareness of self-harming, anorexia, and several other struggles that people face. With her help, we finally had the promotion we needed. The video was set to publish sometime in the afternoon on January 1, 2011. It was perfect. Kayla and I were planning to go to the mountains for New Year's Eve and would be returning later on January 1, just in time for our launch. The only problem was that the video actually published on December 31—a few hours before we were supposed to leave.

When we received word that the video was live, the texts started coming in immediately. Excited and stressed, we did our best to text back with anything that we thought might distract someone from self-harming. We had texts ranging from individuals asking for advice about ways to prevent self-harming, to others simply wanting to talk about anything other than the addiction in order to sway their mind elsewhere.

These feelings of elation were quickly followed up by moments of dread when we realized we were heading up into the mountains where there would be no internet or cell coverage. Anyone who decided to text us wouldn't receive a text back until the following day. It all ended up working out fine, but it was an early lesson in the harsh realities of poor planning.

Nevertheless, we saw the demand and knew we were on to something big. Project Toe was officially born!

For several months, our free texting service grew to the point where it was time to expand and look for volunteers to help us keep up with the demand. We looked for passionate individuals to get on the schedule to help others. When they were scheduled, they would simply log in to the Google Voice account to begin texting people back. We were averaging about 100 new individuals texting in on a monthly basis from around the U.S. at this point. At one point, we had about six active volunteers who would place themselves on the schedule. The volunteers consisted of close friends and people we met through online forums. The majority were young individuals in high school or college who could relate to those texting in. We focused on finding volunteers who could empathize with those that had the urge to self-harm. We believed they were best equipped to prevent others from doing it. This format worked for a while, but it was a challenge trying to manage the volunteers and all the new people texting into our line. It wasn't sustainable and sooner or later things were going to come crashing down. We needed to make a change—only Kayla and I didn't see eye to eye on how we could take Project Toe to the next level. After a few months of tension brewing between Kayla and me, that fateful day finally arrived when the walls came tumbling down.

3

THE ULTIMATUM

Toward the latter part of 2011, everything seemed to be a mess. Kayla and I had a tough time agreeing on anything. We questioned each other's ability, and a growing contempt formed that worsened with each passing day. Project Toe, once something we loved working on together, had become a nightmare.

I finally gave Kayla an ultimatum—either she takes over and I leave, or she leaves and I continue on without her. Regardless, there was no way that we could continue working on this together. It got to the point where our personal relationship was so heavily bruised that our focus had drifted away from what should have mattered—Project Toe.

Without hesitation, she chose to forfeit the reins with no further involvement on her part. Initially, she wanted to continue to be associated, but she knew that idea wouldn't work out, if we continued down our current path.

We both wanted Project Toe to succeed but had conflicting ideas as to how to make that happen. I wanted to focus more on creating an open platform around people helping one another, whereas she envisioned us being the ones to actively recruit the volunteers to represent Project Toe. If I had to make an analogy using YouTube as an example, she wanted to create YouTube videos as a way to create value, whereas I wanted to create the YouTube platform itself. Was her vision bad or the wrong approach? Of course not—it is just that when it comes down to making decisions, the constant battle between us ultimately resulted in us parting ways. In all fairness, it wasn't ever her fault. Looking back, maybe it didn't have to end that way, but our relationship seemed so tainted that it felt like there was no other choice. If Kayla ever reads this, I hope there's a place in her heart for forgiveness. If I had to guess, she loved Project Toe so much that she was willing to abandon her passion in hopes that someday it would grow to be something magnificent. Although she is no longer active, she does remain a co-founder.

It was now time for me to figure out where to take Project Toe. The volunteer approach and the

Google Voice contact method weren't sustainable or scalable. I wanted to open it up so anyone could be a "helper," but first I needed a website. That's when Adam Flowers showed up. He would later become our first technical co-founder.

4

THE WEBSITE

My friendship with Adam Flowers stemmed from a previous start-up we had worked on in college called GoAxum—an online notice board for college students. As a side project, Flowers created a website for Project Toe that would allow anyone to log in either to seek help or to help others. The concept was simple—whenever you had the urge to self-harm, you would click on the link labeled "Toe." Whenever you wanted to help others, you would simply turn on the "Help Others" notification and wait for someone who needed help. On January 1, 2012, the official website launched. Although there were quite a few bugs initially, the site quickly validated my belief that ordinary people are both capable and willing to help one another.

Now we faced an entirely new problem. The "toers," the people who needed help, and the "helpers," the people who wanted to help, both needed to be online at the same time in order for the system to work. We didn't have enough users at the time, however, to make this happen on a consistent basis. The toers would log in and click on "Toe" but would have to wait hours before connecting with someone. Conversely, we learned the helpers had to wait for long periods of time before someone connected with them. This terrible first experience resulted in many first timers not returning. We needed to find a way to speed up the process and to keep both sides engaged long enough to connect.

Around this time, I was living in Paris, France for a semester attending a study abroad program through my school. If anyone has ever considered studying abroad, I would highly recommend it. What amazed me was that the school that I attended only cared about final projects and didn't require class attendance. As you can imagine, this gave me ample time to reflect on Project Toe.

One night, while falling asleep to the sounds of Paris outside my apartment window, I had an epiphany. It was as though someone whispered the words "social therapy" to me, and I quickly scribbled the words in my journal. I felt like I had thought of something that no one else ever had. One week later, while I was researching social therapy on the internet,

I discovered that I was actually *not* the first person to conceive of it—that person was someone by the name of Fred Newman.

5

SOCIAL THERAPY

Fred Newman was an American philosopher, psychotherapist, playwright and political activist, and one of the creators of "social therapy," a term he coined in the 1970s. To sum it up, Fred Newman defined social therapy as mainly "group therapy." In one of his early interviews, he mentioned that social therapy might evolve over time, but admitted that he wasn't quite sure how it would necessarily look.

The internet was not available to the general public at that time and most people did not own a computer. There were no dominant tech companies in the '70s, let alone one based around the mental-health industry. In other words, Fred Newman had this brilliant idea, but he was limited by his environment and what resources were available to him.

When I had conceived of the idea of social therapy that night in Paris, I had never heard of Fred Newman. It wasn't until about one week afterward that I started researching social therapy on the internet. The search results immediately referenced Fred Newman. What caught my eye was the date of his death. Fred Newman died on July 3, 2011, a day or two after I originally thought of the idea of social therapy. It was a weird coincidence. Fred Newman conceived of the original concept that I intended to build off of. Today's resources and infrastructure allow us to instantly connect with anyone. For me, it was unthinkable not to revisit Newman's idea.

At this point in time, we were still using the website, however, it was not performing as well as we had hoped. It would be almost a year, though, before we would finally try to solve our technological challenges with a mobile app. The only problem was that Flowers was strictly a web developer. He didn't know how to build a mobile app, and we didn't have the financial resources to hire someone else to build it.

Months later, I received an unexpected message on Facebook from an acquaintance, Stephen Woodford, that said, "Hey Mike, I really think what you guys are doing with Project Toe is great. I'm not sure if you guys ever considered an iPhone app but I'd love to help out if needed." Some would call it a miracle, while others might refer to it as the Law of Attraction. Little did any of us know at the time that Stephen would end up becoming our second technical co-founder.

6

MOBILE

By this point, most people we knew wondered why we hadn't given up after so many years. After all, Project Toe wasn't making a profit, but our expenses weren't exactly huge either. Our answer was simple; we had a social mission and so we didn't really think about success in the traditional sense of the word. What's the worst that could happen? Maybe we would shut down and decide to try something else. The key would be that we still made an impact on at least one person (or in our case, the thousands we were already serving), ultimately making it worthwhile. That was exactly our mindset then, and it has continued to be as we've grown year after year.

Imagine your own life for a second. Have you ever tried to do something that seemed impossible at first? What was the worst thing that could happen? You might fail. You might accomplish a few goals, but still come up short. Here's the fun part about all of this—even if you "fail," you aren't in a worse position than you were before. Once you realize that, the upside outweighs the downside. When embarking on a new adventure, you'll discover that "failure" doesn't actually exist if you can learn at least one thing that can transfer over to your next project.

Now, with this new opportunity to build an iPhone app, it was time to rethink our approach. One of the major perks of a mobile app is the ability to send push notifications. Push notifications are messages sent automatically from an app to a person's phone, even when that person is not actively using the app. Users would no longer sit for hours waiting to help. They would simply log in to the app, create their Help Schedule, and whenever someone needed to talk, the helpers on call would get a push notification.

On May 22, 2013, we officially launched the iPhone app and have focused on mobile ever since. Finally, everything looked promising again. We were making progress and continuing to receive feedback from users on how we could improve. We systematically made small adjustments over the next year. As we did, I found myself talking to my parents about the Project Toe vision and how it could have an impact on generations to come.

I often spoke to my mother about the project, in particular. She could empathize with those who were going through a serious life struggle, because at the time, she was going through one herself.

7

MOTHER

Ever since my mother was diagnosed with a terminal illness, it became increasingly more difficult for her to move around the house and to see the outside world. She had a disease called pulmonary hypertension, which prevented her from receiving a sufficient amount of oxygen, resulting in her heart working harder than usual. Unfortunately, it's the type of disease that doesn't go away and worsens over time. Although it was a major risk, her only chance for a new lease on life was a double lung transplant at the Cleveland Clinic in Ohio.

In case you have never experienced what it's like to know someone on a waiting list for a new organ, I will tell you it's a bit more complicated than you might initially think. The patient is hoping they'll receive a new organ, however, this needs to happen before his/her body becomes too weak to handle the surgery. If it is determined that the patient is too weak to handle a transplant, they are then taken off the waiting list. Fortunately, my mother eventually received her new lungs. It would ultimately be six months post-surgery before she could finally come home.

She was on the road to recovery. Or so we thought.

At around 5:30 p.m. on May 22, 2014, I came home from work to find my parents watching a movie—something special they would often do together to pass the time. A few hours later, I decided to head out to meet some friends at a local pub:

Me: "Alright Mom, I'm heading out for the night. I'll see you later."

Mom: "Sounds good! Love you, sweetie."

Me: "Yup, love you too!"

Those would be the last words that we would ever exchange.

Later that night, I received an unexpected text message from my father that forever changed the course of my life:

"Come home. Mom's down."

After receiving the text message, I immediately called my father to see what the situation was. He picked up the phone and could barely speak.

Me: "Calm down, Dad. What's wrong?"

Dad: "It's Mom. She's unconscious. The paramedics are giving her CPR. You need to come home now."

I entered the house and saw my dad downstairs on the phone speaking to my brother in California, trying to explain the situation. I immediately went upstairs to see what was happening. As I entered my parents' room, I saw a police officer standing by her and paramedics performing CPR on her as she lay on the ground. I remember feeling this sense of calm as I watched these professionals take control of the situation. The room was silent, and the only sound I heard were what felt like whispers from the paramedics. I quickly came back to reality when the police officer asked if I'd be willing to step into my room for a quick chat.

I sat down as the officer asked me a series of questions about myself—my name, my age, my relationship to her. I quickly interrupted:

Me: "Let's not bullshit."

Officer: "What do you mean?"

Me: "I know that things aren't looking good for her."

It became clear that I was in a state of shock and couldn't quite comprehend my feelings. I was on an emotional roller coaster, feeling sad, angry and confused.

As they carried her out of the front door, I remember this intense thunderstorm that was happening around us. The winds were heavy and it seemed the thunder and lightning wouldn't relent. What was particularly strange was that the weather was completely calm when I first arrived at the house. To this day, my father and I talk about what a bizarre occurrence that was, almost as if the skies opened up.

After the ambulance left, my father and I sat on the floor and tried to make sense of what had happened. I think I said "wow" a few dozen times over the course of 30 minutes. Apparently that's my word of choice after something bad happens and my adrenaline is at full throttle.

Around 1 a.m., I decided to head to the hospital to get some closure. I knew the minute I saw her on the bedroom floor that she was gone, but I needed to hear it from someone else.

During the drive to the hospital, reality finally set in. Suddenly, all my emotions surfaced at once like an overinflated balloon popping. It was a mixture of crying from sadness and screaming with anger. After arriving, it was the classic scene you see in the movies of having to sit in the waiting room until the doctor enters. The doctor finally came in and confirmed that she was gone.

I walked in the operating room where she was lying to say my final goodbyes. The room was dark with one bright light shining over her. As I stood there watching her, silence surrounding the room, I remember thinking to myself how all that I was looking at was her empty shell. Her spirit had left, but her body remained. Is this what death looks like? Is this what we have to look forward to when it's our turn?

It was a dark period in my life, and it took some time to become a functional human being again. Her death opened my eyes to a new perspective on life and a focus on helping people through my work at Project Toe. After she passed away, I needed time to think and reflect. I felt that the only solution was to leave the area to avoid the noise. It was time to return to the city that, for me, always seemed to hold the answers to life's difficult questions.

8

PARIS, FRANCE

Following my mother's death, I decided to rent an apartment for two months in the heart of Paris to take some time to think about my life, Project Toe, and how I wanted to spend my time. My apartment was located in the 8th arrondissement, a few steps away from the Miromesnil metro stop. It was perfectly located to get the full experience of what the city had to offer—close enough to the center to quickly reap the benefits of the city, but far enough away to enjoy the serenity. Now in my ideal environment for creativity, I was able to solidify my thoughts. I kept revisiting three main ideas:

1. We as humans have an innate desire to want to help others.
2. Success and money aren't the same thing.
3. We will all face death at some point in our lives.

We as humans have an innate desire to want to help others.

We are social creatures. We have a need to feel

connected to something or to someone. It hurts to see a harmless individual in pain regardless of whether we have a direct relationship with them or not. Imagine you are walking down the street and witness someone slip and fall. What do you do? Do you continue walking, or do you quickly assist that person to make sure that he or she is okay? Studies suggest that the majority of us would try to make a positive difference in some way. If someone is in need, the majority of us would in fact do something if we had the ability to help. Yes, one might say it's common sense; of course people would want to help. This simple statement, however, is the foundation on which Project Toe is built.

When you combine the idea that we as humans have a desire to want to help others with context (i.e., you can relate to what someone else is going through because you've gone through it yourself), there's suddenly this magical experience for both parties— the person needing help speaks to someone with experience, and the person wanting to help has this emotional drive to be available for this person. Take this idea and combine it with technology, and you suddenly have an opportunity to apply this magical experience to various life struggles that people face from all around the world.

This is how we can expand on the social-therapy concept. Group therapy is part of the social-therapy umbrella, but what we should focus on is recreating that magical energy that happens when you take your own life struggle and leverage that power to better the life of someone who is currently going through the same ordeal. The difference between the 1970s, when Fred Newman first conceived of the idea of social therapy, and now, is, in today's environment, we have the tools to create a platform that makes these connections instantaneously.

Success and money aren't the same thing.

For me, there was much confusion between success and money, and what it meant for Project Toe. If Project Toe was going to succeed and grow, there had to be a mind shift between money and success. When Project Toe began, the focus was on making money in order to achieve success. If Project Toe wasn't making money, I felt like a failure due to my preconceived notion that money was the only metric for success.

Now, it's important to be clear that money helps. Without money, it's extremely difficult to grow a business that helps a growing number of people. Project Toe is a for-profit start-up with a social mission. We decided a long time ago that we didn't want to pursue the non-profit route due to the various constraints that are placed on non-profits (e.g., try incorporating one to start). It's certainly not impossible to run a non-profit, but if we want to significantly improve mental health on a global scale, we need some serious capital, and that capital typically comes from investors who are looking for a return on their investment.

Some of you reading this may be wondering how we could dare call ourselves a "for-profit" when our vision is to empower people to help one another? It seems counterintuitive. Let's try to describe it in a different way. Imagine for a second that you started your own organization around something you are passionate about. Your mission is to help as many people as possible with the resources that you have. You set up a bank account specifically for this organization and invest $1,000 of your own money.

You're doing well, but making slow progress. You are seeing that people are benefiting from your service, but you're slowly running out of money to keep the organization afloat. You definitely don't want to spend money on marketing, because you'll run out of money even faster, but if you don't, how will others find out about you?

You decide to accept donations. You notice that people are willing to donate, but it's typically a one-time occurrence for each individual, and the most someone is willing to donate is between $10 and $20. This is great to sustain your organization, but it's not enough to really take your organization to the next level. One day, you get a donor who's willing to give you $500, but how long will that last before you need to ask for more money?

You then receive an email from someone who has been following your organization. They have an awesome idea that could significantly benefit your users. Since you have a large audience of users, they are willing to give you $20 to promote their service on your website. You promote their service and quickly see the positive feedback from your users. It's a win-win-win situation:

1. The person who paid $20 is happy because of the increased exposure for his or her service.
2. Your users are happy because the promotion offered them something that was relevant to them.
3. You're happy because your users are happy, the organization that you promoted is happy, and you now have $20 that you can reinvest in something else.

Other companies take notice and ask how they too can promote their products and services that also add value to your users. Suddenly, you went from having one organization willing to pay you $20 for a promotion, to 10 companies willing to pay $20 each to do the same thing ($200). Investors start taking notice.

One day, I express my interest in your organization. I see that you have an awesome idea, you're helping a lot of people, and you're making money without going against your own values or the values of those using your service. I invest $10,000 to help bring your organization to the next level. This money helps you reach more people, which increases the number of users, which means outside organizations are willing to pay more to promote their services to your community, ultimately making everyone happy.

If we at Project Toe create enough value for our community and get more healthcare organizations involved, the money will follow. By expressing this concept to potential investors, we did indeed gain access to more capital that will give us the opportunity to make an even bigger impact than if we had gone down the non-profit route. If you're still not sold on the idea that a company can be for-profit and still do good in this world without compromising their values, give us a chance to prove it as we continue to grow.

We will all face death at some point in our lives.

Everyone knows this to be true. My mother's death, however, was a rude awakening that ultimately made me rethink my own life and what really mattered to me.

People who have witnessed someone's death, had someone close to them die, or had a near-death experience, may agree that it changed them in some way. In my case, seeing my mother lying on the floor underscored the following:

1. Death can come unexpectedly.
2. Our lives don't always end when we are "old" as in the case of my mother.
3. Time shouldn't be wasted!

The decision was made in Paris that it was time to raise the bar for Project Toe and for me. While I cannot control my own natural death, I can control what I choose to focus on while I am alive and how I choose to spend my time. I decided to focus on allocating my energy to a subject that I am passionate about (mental health), and continuing to expand Project Toe to help as many people as possible.

When you fully acknowledge and accept the fact that you are only alive for a short period of time, you start to transform yourself from being a passive individual who lets life come his or her way, to an active individual who pursues what he or she really wants.

It's that sense of urgency that we need in order to prosper. I suddenly had a sense of urgency for life after witnessing a loved one's death. I just hope that others can discover this sense of urgency without having to lose someone close to them.

If you need help creating a sense of urgency in your own life, try thinking about it from a different perspective by using the average lifespan of an individual in the U.S.:

1. Average lifespan in U.S.: approximately 80 years

2. Average time spent sleeping (one-third of your life): approximately 26.4 years

3. Average time spent working (one-third of your life): approximately 26.4 years

Most of us think that we will live until we are 80 years old, but if you do the math it's more like 27 years of actual living (if you subtract time spent sleeping and time spent working).

If you want to increase your 27 years of actual living, you can either sleep less—a terrible idea if you're like me—or devote more "working" hours to doing meaningful work.

And yes, you still need to pay the bills. Let me provide an example of how you can convert more of your working hours to meaningful work when working full-time on what you really want to do isn't an option yet.

Years ago, I worked at a job in a field I had no interest in. I took the job because I needed income to live on and to reinvest in Project Toe in order to keep the organization afloat. At the time, I was living at home with low expenses, so from a financial standpoint, I was content. The problem was I wasn't happy. Even though I enjoyed the people I worked with, I felt like what I was doing for eight hours per day didn't align with my long-term interests.

After Paris, I made a commitment to no longer work for companies that didn't align with my interests in mental health and Project Toe, even if it meant foregoing a higher salary. I couldn't necessarily work full-time on Project Toe at the time, but that didn't mean I had to take a job that wouldn't at least get me a little closer.

It took some time, but I was finally able to interview and ultimately obtain a sales position for an amazing tech startup in the mental-health industry called TherapyNotes. It's the best cloud-based practice management website for therapists designed to help them with their note-taking, scheduling, and billing, meanwhile being 100% HIPAA-compliant. Yes, my dream at the time was to work full-time on Project Toe, but the new job aligned with my passion for mental health, which ultimately transferred over to Project Toe during my free time. Suddenly, there was meaning to my work.

If you start looking for work that aligns with your interests or passions, you might be pleasantly surprised to find out where it leads. Oh, and if you don't know what your passions or interests are yet, I have a simple formula for that, as well:

Step 1: Take any job that you think looks interesting and exciting.

Step 2: If it's terrible, after 6 months, quit or look for a new job depending on your financial situation. However, make it a goal to leave no later than the one-year mark, otherwise you're likely to feel stuck with no hope for a better future.

Step 3: Rinse and repeat! Don't settle until you find something insanely awesome. For those who may be younger and who aren't at the "job" stage yet, don't stress! That's one of the perks of taking classes (either through school or free online); classes can help you discover your interests.

9

OUR FUTURE

What does the future hold for Project Toe? In 2015, Project Toe was fortunate enough to receive a substantial amount of capital as an investment that will allow us to take Project Toe to the next level over the next couple of years until we can sustain ourselves financially.

At the time of writing, we currently have seven individuals (including me) working on building out the vision, and are planning on hiring another three individuals over the next few weeks to focus on the Android app. If you've followed Project Toe from the beginning, you'll know that, up until the latter part of 2015, we were mostly focused on those who self-harm. With this funding, our goal is to increase the scope of Project Toe to include other life struggles. The big question is, how do we do this?

Project Toe was always known as an organization. In 2011, we had an idea that we could help a lot of people. As we matured, we realized that the real power of Project Toe wasn't in the technology, but rather in the community—those of you who were willing to make a difference in someone else's life.

We also know that many of you have experienced things that the majority of us cannot fathom, and if only you had the power to help others, you could make a significant impact, as well. As of today, Project Toe is going to allow you to do just that.

Our vision is simple: "To empower people to help one another." For those who want to help on a massive scale, we are going to create the platform that will allow you to create your own support group.

Let's say that you went through a difficult time in your life and you've always wanted to create your own support group around that particular life struggle (similar to what Project Toe did initially), but there wasn't a platform out there that would allow you to do just that? A platform that not only helped you become successful, but also offered you the ability to create something of your own at little to no cost? If you had the resources and the capability to change people's lives for the better, what would you create?

Maybe you'd offer a support group in your local community for those suffering from depression. Maybe you're like me and lost a loved one and want to create a support group around grief. You're only limited by your imagination. Meanwhile, our focus at Project Toe is to figure out how to create the best platform possible to help you do just that. In the end, Project Toe is nothing more than a name. It's people like you—through your willingness to take the time to help others—who ultimately deserve the credit. It's people like you—through your effort to help others and make the world a better place—who are taking the name "Project Toe" and turning it into a community.

Yes, along the way, we are going to make mistakes—some will be minor while others may cause small setbacks. Just like for those facing a difficult time in life, it's always easier when you have a support group. We are asking you to be our supporters as we continue to build Project Toe. I can't promise that Project Toe will be around forever. In the end, Project Toe is a start-up with a social mission and a dream of possibly revolutionizing the mental-health industry. Unfortunately, you may be reading this when Project Toe is no longer in existence. But that's okay. As you may recall from the quote at the beginning of this book:

"If you want to find the best ideas that could change the world, look no further than the graveyard."

I didn't write this book to talk only about Project Toe. I wrote this book because I didn't want to be someone who had an idea but never shared it with anyone. There are too many lives at stake to bring this idea to the grave. Regardless of whether Project Toe is around by the time you read this or not, I hope this idea of social therapy inspires you to take action in some way, big or small. If you are able to use your past experience to help someone currently going through a life struggle, then I feel as though at least we accomplished something together.

I also wrote this book so that you could get to know me. Throughout this book, I wanted to let you in on my life and to share my values with you. As Project Toe continues to grow, transparency and openness will be even more vital, as its success boils down to trust. Project Toe may have great intentions, but if you don't trust the leadership behind the name, Project Toe can only do so much. I made a decision that no matter what it is that I'm doing, I want to be as open and transparent as possible to those who wish to get to know me (you'll understand why in the final chapter).

It was very difficult to open up and to write about the night of my mother's death. Although her death was unexpected, she knew from the beginning that she may not live long enough to watch her friends and family grow up. It was a reality that she had accepted.

After her death, my family was sorting through her things, and we found envelopes with letters inside addressed to each of us. We quickly realized that these weren't just any letters—they were goodbye letters that she wrote several months prior. As I looked at the envelope with my name on it, it made me wonder if she knew, if she knew that things weren't going to work out according to plan. I went to my room alone to read the letter with tears in my eyes. Her letter consisted of all the positive memories and fun times that we had together growing up. There was one part of the letter that I found most surprising though. Within the letter, she expressed to me how she viewed my personality (the good and the bad). If there's any content out there that would provide an authentic and raw perspective of one's own life, it would be a loved one's final words before passing.

I would like to honor her by devoting the last chapter to the final words that she wrote to me. If there's one person who truly knew me, it was she. Transparency and trust are important to me, and sharing this letter, although not easy, will hopefully help you make a difference to someone just as much as she made a difference to me. Her letter has not been altered in any way.

After you read her letter, I'd like you to think

about your own life and the ways that you may be able to make a difference to someone. If it's related to a past struggle or life event that you have experienced, there's a good chance that there's a support group on Project Toe that you could join to offer your support should someone need it. If you can help at least one person, you'll start to question how strong you really are. If you continue helping others, something magical will happen. It will make you rethink your own life's purpose, and you'll start to ask yourself one of the most powerful questions there is:

"What else am I capable of?"

10

"MIKE"

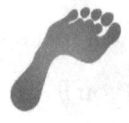

Mike,

- Thoughtful
- Intuitively knows what's up
- Good heart
- Planner
- Hard worker
- Consistent
- Keeps things to himself – very private
- Deep thinker
- Holds self to tough standards and high ideals

When you were born we were in transition so you lived in a snuggle against my heart. You were so good all of the time. We went on the Metro everyday looking for houses in France. Poor Mark usually had to walk. You weren't much of a talker for a long time. You always were a deep thinker though because so many times we couldn't figure out what you were saying and finally when we could understand it was "wow." You blew us away. We couldn't believe such a little guy was capable of such deep thoughts. You were always thinking too. I said we were going to the mall, you knew right away (you were about 2 years old) that there was a merry-go-round with a motorcycle so you ran upstairs and got your helmet. It was great!

Remember our neat backyard in France? It was tiny but it had a pergola with lights running all along the back. Your slide/climbing thing was in one corner. You got it for your birthday. We had a built-in grill and a really cool spigot for water. Because our house used to be a model home it had lots of extras. Like the white fireplace and white carpets, the designer kitchen where our refrigerator had a cabinet door so it blended with the other cabinets. It was a neat house. Then when we moved to the U.S we wanted you to have a big U.S birthday so we had it at Aunt Tish's with a pony to ride. We had hats and bandanas. It was really fun.

Remember before our neighbors house was built, we'd have picnics on the little hill? We felt like we could just eat and look around at the neighborhood all day. Our dog, Carver, loved to come too.

Remember how easily you learned to drive your brothers fire engine? You were usually the passenger but you were ready when you got your chance.

Remember your first motorcycle? Or was it a quad? The blue electric vehicle. Later you bought that Harley bicycle. You were riding a two-wheeler so early. Were you 3 years old? Your brother knew you could do it so he got your training wheels off and away you went.

Your fascination with planes was so interesting to us. Where did it come from at such a young age?

With your college experiences you are well on your way to being successful in business. You just jump in and start. That's a real strength and I give you credit.

You have so many good qualities that will serve you well in life. A good heart, a hard worker, and you are interested in so many things.

Take time for yourself because that is what will ground you and keep you sane. Remember that I believe in you and will love you always!

Love, Hugs & Kisses,

Mom ♥

THE END

How many lives can you help?

ProjectToe.com

THE WORD "TOE"

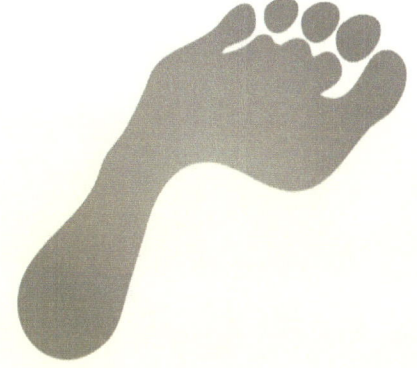

THE WORD "TOE"

www.ingramcontent.com/pod-product-compliance
Lightning Source LLC
Chambersburg PA
CBHW022345290526
45786CB00014B/2504